P9-DBS-987

SELLING

WHAT EVERY SUCCESSFUL SALES PROFESSIONAL
NEEDS TO KNOW

ZIG ZIGLAR

THOMAS NELSON PUBLISHERS®
Nashville

A Division of Thomas Nelson, Inc.
www.ThomasNelson.com

Published in Nashville, Tennessee, by Thomas Nelson, Inc.

Library of Congress Cataloging-in-Publication Data

Ziglar, Zig.
Selling 101 / Zig Ziglar.
p. cm.
Includes bibliographical references.
ISBN 10: 0-7852-6481-7 (hardcover)
ISBN 13: 978-0-7852-6481-1
1. Selling. 2. Success in business. I. Title: Selling one hundred one.
II. Title.
HF5438.25 .Z542 2003
658.85—dc21
2002151311

Printed in the United States of America

08 09 10 WOZ 17

Dedicated
to
all enthusiastic and honorable sales professionals
who sell goods, products, or services
that benefit others

CONTENTS

Is This Book for You?

Many years ago Aristotle said that if you took two weights of the same material, the one that was the larger of the two would fall faster. For years this was taught at the University of Pisa. Many years later Galileo came along and said that simply was not true. When his opinion was challenged by the students, he went to the top of the Leaning Tower of Pisa, dropped two weights dramatically different in size but of the same material, and they hit the ground at precisely the same time. Galileo had proved his point, but interestingly enough, at the University of Pisa they kept teaching that the heavier weight would fall faster. Here's why: He had *convinced* the students he was right, but he had not *persuaded* them.

The question in the world of sales is: How do you persuade? Answer: You don't persuade by telling, you persuade by asking. A large portion of *Selling 101* is devoted to asking questions, with emphasis on listening for the answers. Those of you who read the Bible know (and whether you are a believer or not most people respect the fact) that Christ was a powerful persuader. I encourage you to go to a good bookstore, buy a red-letter edition of the Bible (because the words of Christ are printed in red), and read. You will make an amazing discovery, namely, that when people asked Christ a question He either responded with a question or a parable—both of which are tools for persuasion.

My best friend (he's really more a brother) for the last thirty-seven years is of the Jewish faith and is from Winnipeg, Canada. I noticed this questioning characteristic in him, and I asked him one time why he always answered a question with a question. He smilingly said, "Well, why not?" Asking the right question and listening to the answer is a great relationship builder, which is important to the persuasion process.

The second underlying and overlying message in *Selling 101* is the importance of integrity in building a sales career. With integrity you do the right thing—that eliminates any guilt. With integrity you have nothing to fear because you have nothing to hide. Now, with fear and guilt removed, you have the freedom to be the person God created you to be. I say this because we are trained to persuade. A salesperson without integrity is inclined to overstate the benefits and persuade people to buy overpriced products they neither need nor really want. Selling with integrity is the only way you can build a long-term career with the same company selling the same product to the same people—which brings sales stability and financial security.

Laurel Cutter, Vice Chairman of FCB Leber Katz Partners, says: "Values determine behavior; behavior determines reputation; reputation determines advantages." Start building your reputation of integrity today and I will *See You Over The Top!*

Zig Ziglar

I

You Made the Right Choice

Attitude is always a "player" on your team.

Welcome to *Selling 101!* I would like to begin in a somewhat unusual manner. Let me encourage you to leave the sales profession if you can. Yes, you read it properly. Zig Ziglar is encouraging you to quit selling—if you can. Those last three words are the most important words you can face at this point in your sales career: *if you can*. Those who get into sales because they might make a little more money or might even help other people are "short-termers." You need to get into selling because your heart and your head won't allow you to do anything else!

In sales, you will be treated rudely. People will, on occasion, even slam doors in your face. They will hang up on you for no obvious reason. Some will avoid you at social gatherings. Your family (and even *you*) will question your sanity. As humorist and speaker Dr. Charles Jarvis says, "Just because you're paranoid doesn't mean they're not out to get you!" Yes, paranoia can be a side effect of the sales profession.

Are You In?

My good friend Walter Hailey is one of the most successful men in the world. Walter is a salesman par excellence (that means he's gooood!) and a winner who has spent his life helping others win.

Despite Walter's success, he had a rocky start in the world of selling. He faced frustration, anxiety, closed doors, low sales, nervous stomach, and virtually every other symptom associated with an individual who is uncertain of how he is going to survive in the sales world. As a matter of fact, his discouragement was so bad, Walter went to his manager and told him he was quitting, getting out of the business. To this his manager responded, "You can't."

Walter dogmatically stated again that he was quitting. His manager replied, "Walter, you can't get out of the insurance business because you have never really gotten into the insurance business."

Walter said the words hit him like the proverbial "ton of bricks." As he reflected on the truth of what his manager said, he realized for possibly the first time in his life that *you cannot get out of something you have never been in*. There are many people who "join" a sales organization but never get in the business of selling. Please understand that you may have been presenting your product or service for years and still not have been "in the profession" of selling.

Lack of commitment is a primary reason that the sales profession has earned the reputation for having a high turnover rate. Fortunately, this is changing, and the public is rapidly gaining respect for the true sales professional.

My Journey to Sales Success

I have a deep love for the sales profession and the selling professional, a sincere belief in the value of our profession, and an unquenchable thirst for knowledge about becoming even more professional.

My sales career didn't begin in 1947 with my first "official" sales call. It actually started in childhood when I sold vegetables on the streets of Yazoo City, Mississippi. I also had a paper route, and early in my sales career it was my good fortune to work in a grocery store for several years.

At the University of South Carolina I sold sandwiches at the dormitory in the evenings to finance my marriage and education. I later moved into direct sales that have included stints in the securities business, life insurance, and home care products. I entered the world of personal growth and corporate development in 1964 and have been selling training and motivation since then.

THE BENEFITS ARE FOR YOU!

Let me encourage you to begin each day with this statement: "Today I will be a successful sales professional, and I will learn something today that will make me even more professional tomorrow." If you remind yourself of this commitment daily, then many benefits await you as a successful sales professional!

INDEPENDENCE

One of the many great benefits about our profession is that you are truly your own boss. You are in business, as the saying goes, "for yourself but not by yourself." When you stand in front of the mirror each morning, you can look yourself right in the eye and say, "My goodness, you're such a nice, efficient, effective, hardworking, and professional person—you deserve a raise!" and the board just met. I might add that the raise will become effective as soon as you do.

OPPORTUNITIES

In short, with the independence of being your own boss comes a tremendous responsibility, and this is the exciting part of the profession! *Opportunity is born of independence handled in a responsible manner*, and in the sales profession, your opportunities are unparalleled.

Problem Solving

With the possible exceptions of medicine and the ministry, no one is in as good a position to solve problems as you, the professional persuader. There is virtually nothing on earth that brings as much personal satisfaction and gratification as being able to save another human being a considerable amount of time, money, frustration, and/or anxiety because of the goods, products, or services you have to offer.

Security

Of course, I'd be less than honest if I didn't confess that the high-income potential offered in the profession of selling is a tremendous lure. Both money and advancement are attractive to those who are ambitiously dissatisfied with having low ceilings established on their worth and activities, and for those who are tired of being dependent on the whims of other people incapable of making objective evaluations about their worth. But security is an "inside" job. In sales you don't have to wait for things to happen; you can make things happen. When business is slow, you can go out and stir the marketplace and get it into action. You can have greater control of your life and your future, and THAT is a secure feeling, especially for your family!

FAMILY

My wife is a decided redhead, meaning one day she just "decided" to be a redhead, so when I talk about her, I call her "the Redhead" (and she enthusiastically encourages me to do so). When I'm talking to her, I call her Sugar Baby. Her name is Jean.

From the beginning of my marriage to the Redhead, through the rearing of our children—Suzan, Cindy, Julie, and Tom—each has been intimately involved in considerable detail in every aspect of my sales career. They have shared the excitement, the glory, the benefits, the fun, and yes, the frustrations and anxieties that come with the profession of selling. My family has been privileged to go on trips to beautiful convention areas and reap the benefits of sharing the limelight when trophies and awards were earned. They were also there when I was in a sales slump and needed their support and encouragement. Actually, those times drew us as close as (if not closer than) the times when things were going wonderfully well.

Be honest with the family. They want to "feel" and "be" a part of trials and triumphs. They can be a source of strength and encouragement, and in the process, their own growth into maturity will be enhanced. This great profession enabled us, as a family, to have more shared interests, develop more mutual friends, and broaden our scope of life and living by associating with other people who were excited about selling and the products and services they were able to offer.

Moving Up

Another benefit of being a sales professional is moving up. Salespeople consistently move into the executive suites because of the increasing depth and breadth of skills they must acquire. They must be creative and open as well as flexible in thinking. They have to come up with a creative way to solve problems almost *as* they make their presentation and while adapting to fit the prospect's needs and desires.

Salespeople also encounter people at every emotional level—when they're happy, excited, and enthusiastic; and when they're irritated and down in the dumps—which is tremendous preparation for a spot in the executive suite. The better we get at those "people skills," the more likely we are to move into the upper echelons of management.

Obviously, sales professionals also must know how to persuade others if they're going to convince people to buy, and these skills transfer to corporate headquarters. Considerable skill is required to encourage people to cooperate, to work with other people in the organization, and to persuade them that even when they feel their idea is best, once that idea has been rejected and someone else's inserted, the good, ambitious employee will lay aside personal whims and cooperate for the good of the team. And believe me when I say this task requires great persuasion skills, commitment, and discipline.

ARE YOU WITH ME?

If you can't imagine living without the wonderful benefits our great profession offers, then *congratulations!* You just joined the profession that has the power to dramatically affect and empower our society in a way that many other professions cannot.

2

IMPORTANT SKILLS FOR TODAY'S SALES PROFESSIONAL

A primary reason I have worked so hard to grow Ziglar Training Systems into an internationally respected training company is so that we can SELL each other on the importance of the foundation stones of honesty, character, integrity, faith, love, and loyalty. In order to build on these foundations, we need to develop skills for learning, listening, communicating, and becoming dependable and credible. With these skills, we can build a business, a life, a family, a friendship, and a professional selling career while making a difference in the world in which we live.

HONESTY AND INTEGRITY IN SELLING

Making a difference in the world depends upon honesty and integrity. Being ethical is not only the right way to live; it is also the most practical way to live. True selling professionals don't talk about ethics; they LIVE ethically!

INTEGRITY, HONESTY, AND ETHICS PAY OFF

When Robert Davis was an outstanding salesman and sales manager for Terminix Pest Control in Baton Rouge, Louisiana, if you asked what he did for a living, he'd simply respond, "I kill bugs." His healthy self-esteem and belief in his company's services allowed him to excel personally and professionally.

At one point in his career with Terminix, Robert had a new salesman who got a little overzealous. Late one Friday afternoon, a client called with a serious problem. Bees were swarming around his home and placing the family in distress. Robert assigned his new man to the seemingly simple task, but as the salesman headed out the door, he called back, "Has anyone ever sold a $200 'bee job'?" The others smiled at his "bravado" and said, "No."

When the new man returned in less than thirty minutes with a check for $225, everyone was quite amazed. The telephone interrupted the excitement that bringing in a check for the largest "bee job" ever was generating. Robert answered, and the man who had signed the check was on the phone.

"I just wanted to call and thank you for responding so quickly and getting rid of my problem," the man began. "Those bees were a real concern, and your man certainly did the job."

"But I was wondering," he continued, "if $225 was normal for a fifteen-minute job."

"Are you going to be home for the next few minutes?" was Robert's immediate response. When he got an affirmative answer, Robert put the salesman and the check in his car. When they arrived at the man's home, Robert walked right up to the man and said, "Sir, I'm afraid we got a little carried away with our enthusiasm. Since I had not clearly explained the parameters of this job and how it should be billed to our new salesman, we overcharged you. (Notice that he did nothing to embarrass the salesman, though he had in fact explained exactly how to do the job and said that it was a $125 job at the most.) So this one's on us." With that, he handed the man his check.

"Well, that's mighty kind of you," the man said, "but I still have this problem with roaches and ants. Can you do that for me at no charge, too?"

They all laughed, even as Robert wrote out the contract for the $300 sale that resulted from his ethics, integrity, and honesty. Had they kept the check for the "record" (and unfair) bee job, they would have had a client who wondered if he had been "ripped off." By their returning the money and doing the right thing, Robert's company was rewarded with a larger sale *and* a long-term client.

When you are honest and ethical and live with integrity,

your rewards are guaranteed. They may not happen as quickly as they did for Robert Davis, but just like putting money in the bank guarantees a return, demonstrating the qualities of honesty, integrity, and ethical behavior will guarantee a positive return in your career.

TRUST

The one thing that customers have *always* rated highest in the sales world is *trust*, which is a direct reflection on the integrity of the individual. The primary reason people will choose *not* to buy from you is lack of *trust*. When you make a serious promise to the prospect or a "casual comment" involving a promise, the prospect takes both as gospel. This is especially true if there is any difficulty during the sales process and even after the sale. If the person has any trouble in any phase of the relationship or use of the product, there is the distinct possibility that any "lack of follow-through" will be blown completely out of proportion. Even the tiniest matters become "deal shattering."

LISTENING

All successful sales professionals utilize listening skills to their fullest. Thus far in my career, I have never heard of anyone missing a sale because of listening to the prospect's needs, wants, and desires. Interestingly enough, the more sales-people know about their prospects' needs, the better position they are in to meet those needs. Not only that, but the trust factor goes up when the prospects see salespeople intensely listening to their needs and desires.

Listening is just *not* as difficult as we make it. When we are *not* talking or *preparing* to talk, we can listen. There are many steps and even week-long courses in developing listening skills, but for our needs here we can use the old saying, "Talking is sharing, but listening is caring."

RECIPROCITY

When we carefully "listen" to the prospect's elaborate interests, desires, hobbies, and other thoughts, we are putting them in debt to us. They then have a feeling they "owe" us something, and consequently, they are more willing to "listen" to our story since we have given them the courtesy of listening to them.

COMMUNICATION SPECIFICS

Most people like to listen at the same speed they speak, so whenever possible adjust your speech patterns to conform to those of the prospect. Some exceptions to this policy are the following:

1. The prospect "loses his cool" and gets loud and abusive. When anger enters the picture, lower your voice and slow your rate of speech.

2. The prospect uses crude or profane language. Keep your language clean and professional. Chances are excellent that the prospect will judge you by a higher standard than he judges himself. The higher the level of moral dignity and integrity, the higher the level of trust and respect. The higher the level of trust and respect, the better your chances of making the sale.

3. The prospect speaks so quietly you must strain to hear every word. Keep your voice level at a comfortable volume so you are certain you are being heard. The prospect will not work as hard to understand you as you will to understand him.

4. The prospect speaks so agonizingly slow or so incredibly fast that if you emulate him or her completely, the distraction would be obvious. You should make some adjustment in the direction of the prospect's speech pattern.

5. Never conform to speech accents, bad grammar, slang, or speech impediments.

Dependability and Credibility

Sheila West, author of *Beyond Chaos*, helped me understand the woman's perspective in sales when she said, "The most difficult part for a woman in sales (or many other fields) is to gain credibility. It is impossible for women to do this without being dependable. Therefore, the ones who do not have this trait are washed out of the field quickly. In other words, their dependability gives them credibility, and believability becomes confidence, and with confidence comes success!" This lesson is important for both men and women in the sales profession.

TODAY'S SALES PROFESSIONAL

The successful sales professional knows that happiness is not pleasure, it is victory; that when you do what you need to do when you need to do it, you will eventually be able to do what you *want* to do when you want to do it. And most important, the successful sales professional *knows* and *understands* the sales credo: *You can have everything in life you want if you will just help enough other people get what they want!*

3

FINDING SOMEONE
WILLING TO BUY

The consensus among outstanding salespeople and sales trainers is almost unanimous: Prospecting is the most important key to sales success! It is true that a journey of a thousand leagues begins with but a single step, and it is equally true that until you have a prospect, you have no chance of making a sale.

Someone once facetiously remarked, "The only problem with making a sale is the fact that you just lost your best prospect!" Obviously, this is true, but when you replace that prospect with several more, you have actually won twice.

WHAT?

What is a prospect? A prospect is an individual or a group capable of making the decision on the product or service the salesperson is selling. There is obviously a difference between a "prospect" and a "suspect." A "suspect" is a name that *could* be a prospect, so the name offers hope. But unless that hope has a solid foundation, you have only a suspect. A "prospect" has a need for the product, a possible desire to own that product, and the financial capacity to implement that decision. You "spend" time with suspects; you "invest" time with prospects.

WHEN?

So the question becomes, When do people prospect? The answer is, *All the time!* Prospecting is not an eight-to-five job. Prospecting, when done graciously, can be done in virtually any environment—in social situations, on an airplane, in an airport, at a luncheon or a club meeting, or *whenever people are present.*

I encourage you to remember your ABP's—that is, "Always Be Prospecting." Regularly get out of the circle you're in and start another circle or another chain. Use all your resources to keep those prospect lists long and diverse so that your career is not dependent on one individual or one specific group of individuals.

HOW?

The best way to begin prospecting is to display a genuine interest in the other person, which brings us back to an oft-made point. When you're the right kind of person, your chances of becoming an effective salesperson are much, much better. Here's what I mean. My mother and my wife would rebel at the thought that they could be very successful sales-people since neither ever "officially sold" any goods, products, or services. Yet each of them would have been superb because they're the greatest natural "friend makers" I've ever seen.

My mother could get aboard a bus for a trip, and by the time she reached her destination, she would have made a life-long friend with the person seated next to her. They would correspond with each other for years. She had a *genuine interest in* and *concern for* other people. The same is true of the Redhead. When we're aboard an airplane or, for that matter, waiting in a line at the airport or in a hotel to check in, the chances are excellent *something* will happen—the con-versational door will be opened, and thirty seconds later the Redhead will be engaged in a conversation that would lead you to believe a lifetime friendship already existed. I am fas-cinated and in awe of the way this happens.

WHO?

May I ask you a few questions? With whom do you commu-nicate most often? With whom do you communicate most effectively? Why do you spend so much time selling every-body but the people you know best?

When first asked that question, I was stumped for an answer. After giving it some thought, I reacted by saying, "Well, I wouldn't want my friends and family to think I am pushing my product on them."

The question I had to answer then, and you must answer now, is, If you think your product is good enough for all those strangers, why isn't it good enough for your friends and your family?

If what you are selling is not good enough for your friends and family, then why are you selling it? If it is good, then why would you want to keep it from those you care about most? I understand that there are organizations that encourage you to sell friends and relatives and then drop you like the proverbial "hot potato." But you are mature enough to know (or you wouldn't be reading this book) that you are not going to sell for this type of organization.

What Should I Do?

Many considering selling as a profession write to me to ask how they can be sure they are getting into the right field. The answer is discovered in the area of family and friends. What product or service would you want to offer to your parents, brothers and sisters, friends, acquaintances, and others with whom you come in contact? I strongly encourage those in the world of selling to deal with a product or service *they cannot help talking about!*

You should remind friends and family that you're offering your product or service because you sincerely believe their interests are best served by buying. This must be done with tact, but the key is your conviction that you really are offering something that will strengthen the friendship or relationship because of the value of your offer. However, you don't expect them to buy (and won't permit them to buy) because they are your friends and want to "help" you. You don't build a career that way, but you *do* kill friendships that way.

An additional advantage to offering your services to close friends and relatives is that they will have a serious interest in your success and will be delighted to open doors for you to the best prospects of all.

SPECIFIC HOW-TOS

How do you ask for prospect referrals? Try following these steps:

STEP ONE

Professionals have been asking their prospects and clients for many years, "Mr. Smith, if your best friend were to walk in here at this moment, would you introduce him to me?" The odds are about four thousand to one the answer will be yes. "Then, Mr. Smith, let me get you to do this. Why not introduce me to your best friend who has a need for our services by giving me his name and a little information about him?" You have just taken step one in developing a center of influence.

STEP TWO

If the person who is your center of influence is thoroughly sold on what you do and has benefited from your services, ask him if he will introduce you to the friend via the telephone. A nice alternative to the phone call is a short note saying something like, "John, my friend Bill has something that will benefit you."

STEP THREE

My personal experience tells me that when I am prospecting, I should never place several prospect cards (information cards with a place for name, address, etc.) in front of the client and ask for names. Many times the customer gets a mental block. Always start by asking for one prospect, and *you* write that person's name on a card. At that point do not attempt to get any information concerning that particular prospect. Go for the second, third, fourth, and fifth names. When the "referrer's" well has apparently run dry, go back to prospect number one and get the vital information about address, employment, phone number, responsibilities, general interests and activities.

Step Four

In prospecting please remember that all of us frequently need a little memory jogging. You can accomplish this by asking a few questions: "With whom do you jog, play bridge, work, go to club meetings or church? Who are your neighbors, classmates, etc.?"

Step Five

Once you've got your prospects, ask the "referrer" which person you should call on first, and work with the client to establish a priority list for your names. You will also obtain some "qualifying" information (knowledge about the prospect's ability to buy). Remember to report back to your "referrers" and let them know the results of your calls. Keeping satisfied clients informed is good public relations and good selling, and it makes good sense. Even more important, it solidifies your relationship with your client and keeps the door and his mind open to giving you more prospects.

WHERE TO FIND PROSPECTS

Suppose you're brand new. You picked up this book and your sample kit on the same day, and you don't have Prospect Number One. Where do you start? Answer: You begin by opening your eyes and observing *everything* around you! You will notice that in your office there are customer files with which you can begin working. Chances are excellent that your trainer and your company will be willing and anxious to share this information with you so you can start making those contacts on the service-and-referral concept as your beginning point.

Whether beginning or experienced, professional salespeople use a technique known as "eagle-eye prospecting." By carrying a tape recorder as you drive around, you can "sight" possible prospects. Billboards, storefronts, advertising—anything that looks like a legitimate prospect can be recorded. Later you can look up details (addresses, phone numbers, etc.).

Reference sources like Dun & Bradstreet provide data about the basic business, CEO's name, number of employees, and the approximate volume of business. For more information go to: Zapdata.com.

The library has a source book called *Contacts Influential: Commerce and Industry Directory*, which will have businesses in a particular market area listed by name, type of business, key personnel, etc. If you are going from one business to the next, you will have the advantage of knowing the name of every business on that street, plus the name of the CEO.

The Chamber of Commerce and the Better Business Bureau also have sources of pertinent information. If you are an "in-home" salesperson, you can get information from many power and light companies about the new services they've installed. The newspapers print announcements that will provide prospects if you will carefully screen them. New births indicate a need for baby products and additional insurance. Weddings-to-be open the door for bridal services, clothing, furniture, insurance, travel services, and hotel or motel accommodations for the upcoming event. Executive promotions could mean prospects for larger homes, expanded wardrobes, club memberships, investment programs, automobiles, personal computers, and numerous other items. The possibilities are limited only by your imagination—and your powers of observation.

RELATED INDUSTRIES

Remember that related industries can be companions *to* and prospects *for* the products you sell. It's a natural relationship to establish and can be mutually advantageous to form a marketing team, supplying each other with prospects.

A communications-systems sales associate of mine began

networking with another person who was also selling communications but offered a completely different service. They were a great complement to each other—regardless of who saw the client first.

HELPFUL HINTS IN FINDING PROSPECTS

How long do you wait before you go to see the new prospect? There is something about the psychology of a brand-new prospect, especially if he's just been given to you by an enthusiastic customer. I encourage you to go with all possible haste to see that individual. A week later you won't be nearly as enthused about the prospect. Even though the prospect's needs might not have changed and he might have no earthly idea that he's even on your list, the fact is that you will be less enthused about him, which means you will be less effective in your presentation to him.

IN CLOSING

Now that you know how to find those "willing buyers," what are you going to do? If you said, "Make the sales call," you answered properly. However, some fail to take action. The following chapter on overcoming call reluctance will help you follow through on your "good intentions."

4

DEALING EFFECTIVELY WITH
CALL RELUCTANCE

Few who join the proud profession of selling avoid the anxious and excited feelings that accompany the sales call. But the good news is that *you* can join the group of achievers who overcame call reluctance by using the feeling of anxiety to work *for* you instead of against you. As my friends in the outstanding speaking organization Toastmasters International are fond of saying, "You will not get rid of the butterflies, but you can get them flying in formation."

As a matter of fact, if you feel no anxiety in making the sales call, your chances of success will be greatly diminished. When healthy and functioning properly, the human body is equipped with an endocrinological system that provides every chemical necessary to be successful in life. When we are anxious, the pituitary gland secretes adrenaline, which increases our mental and physical capacity. Realizing that your anxiety is a positive factor, not a negative factor, allows you to focus on the most important factor in call reluctance—*you!*

According to sales experts, 84 percent of all salespeople

have call reluctance to some degree. This fear is manifested in many different ways, but *procrastination* is the number one indication that a problem is developing. When the salesperson creates nonessential tasks that must be done before going out to face the public, call reluctance is setting in.

In many ways, fear of facing the public has a great deal to do with self-image. Until the salesperson learns to "look up to" or "down upon" no person, fear will prevail. Regarding your product or service, *you are the expert.* You have more experience, more knowledge, and more expertise than the prospect will ever have in your area. Mediocre performance is the order of the day until the salesperson becomes a sales professional by realizing that each individual has strengths.

Building Confidence

One of the best ways to recognize your strengths is to replay the tapes on your mind's "video player" of the times you were successful. Everyone needs this "accomplishment feedback." Go back to any and all successful experiences: a big sale; a winning performance in the orchestra, the band, or athletics; a time when you and your family experienced a feeling of love and togetherness; an event where you were recognized for exceptional performance. The next time you feel self-doubt creeping in, replay this vivid, positive tape.

Next, recognize that no matter how successful, wealthy, or powerful your prospect may be, that person makes mistakes just like you and I do. No one has been 100 percent successful in life. As a general rule, my experience is that the more successful the person becomes, the more obstacles, mistakes, and hurts have been overcome. When you realize that the prospect is human, you are less likely to be intimidated.

THE PROPER FOCUS

The second way to alleviate anxiety is to understand that *selling is a transference of feeling*. After learning to focus on *you* so that you may improve your self-concept in a positive manner, you need to recognize that the most successful sales professionals make a sales call with the *prospect* as the center of their focus. Money can be a motivating (and necessary) factor—after all, if you don't prosper financially, you don't stay in business—but when you go into the sales call strictly for the money, you will leave that call without the sale more often than not.

When you place the focus *only* on the money, or if you're in the financial position of *having* to make the sale, you will instinctively press too hard or become overly conscious of your need, putting undue pressure on yourself and increasing your feelings of anxiety.

Successful sales professionals make the sales call for the benefit of the prospect *and* for their personal gain—*in that order*. You see, *you can have everything in life you want if you will just help enough other people get what they want.* Keeping this statement in mind is the third step in overcoming anxiety.

TELEPHONE TERROR

The salesperson who is *competent* in the use and understanding of the telephone and is *confident* of having that competence is going to be a far more *effective* salesperson than the one who is "afraid" of the telephone.

One of the greatest causes of phone fear is failing to set an objective for the call. Are you going to do a market survey, make an appointment, or get the sale? Until you have that clear-cut picture in your mind, your *willingness* to "smile and dial" is going to be seriously limited. Please don't look past this seemingly simple but significant point: *Determine why you are making the call!*

In all the years I've been in selling I don't remember ever looking forward with excitement to what many salespeople have come to refer to as "the cold call." However, I knew that once I got into the swing of things and made several calls, I was getting closer and closer to the sale. With that in mind, I gave no further thought to making the call. I set my time to get started, and at precisely that time I started.

THE BEST TIME TO CALL

A tip you might find helpful when you are having extreme difficulty in reaching your contact is to make your calls early in the morning. (Obviously, this suggestion is made for calling business offices only. Making business calls to individuals at home early in the morning is a sure-fire way to lose a sale.) Many times the decisionmakers will answer the phone at 6:30, 7:00, or 7:30 in the morning. Their energy levels are high and, generally speaking, they're more gracious and willing to listen. Equally important, they respect—even admire—someone with a work ethic similar to their own.

On occasion you will reach a person who will respond to the question "Do you have a few moments we can talk?" with, "I really don't, but go ahead and tell me what's on your mind." I encourage you not to rush into the presentation because you will probably have to speed through and leave out some relevant details. This leads to a snap decision, and in many cases it's not the one you want. I urge you to set a later time to call back. What you have to say about your product should be too important for you to be willing to give out incomplete information that would not adequately prepare your prospect to make a decision.

Along these same lines, if you hear a lot of paper shuffling while you're in the process of making a presentation, or if there's other undue noise in the background, obviously the prospect is not giving you his undivided attention. Be sensitive to what your prospect is saying and is *not* saying. The first few seconds you're on the phone will set the stage, mood, and atmosphere of the presentation, so have a plan.

DRESS FOR SUCCESS OVER THE PHONE

Even if you're working from home or a spot where you know you will not be seen by anyone, are you properly dressed? Did you take a shower this morning? Shave? Apply your makeup? In short, did you really get physically dressed for the call? The evidence is overwhelming that to be mentally sharp you need to be physically sharp. It will make a difference in the expression on your face and the expectancy in your mind, and there'll be a difference in your voice.

Have you given yourself a good sales self-talk? Have you reminded yourself that you're a winner, that you're on an important mission, that as you dial people they will eagerly anticipate your call? Do you visualize them responding favorably to what you're going to say? When you do these things, your results will be dramatically better.

SUCCESSFUL CALLS REQUIRE PLANNING AND PREPARATION

To be the winner you are capable of becoming, you must *plan* to win; you must *prepare* to win; and then you have every right to *expect* to win.

Have you ever noticed how much better you feel about yourself when you have a plan of action? You must remember that the will to win is nothing without the will to prepare to win. What are your plans for the day, week, month, year, career? I have never met a salesperson who would not want to sell more with less time and effort. Selling more is possible only when extra effort is expended in the area of preparation.

Preparation and training include taking the information you receive from an outside source and adapting it to fit your situation, learning it so thoroughly that it becomes your own, and then applying those procedures and techniques in the field. Preparing for the day also can include reading some of this book (or any other book) or listening to part of a sales training seminar or recording.

Research by Forest Tennant, M.D., Ph.D., shows that regular doses of motivation will increase your success. Dr. Tennant, one of the top drug experts in the world, has been a consultant for the NFL, NASCAR, the Los Angeles Dodgers, Abbott Laboratories, Texaco, and many others.

Dr. Tennant attended a seminar I conducted in Anaheim, California. Before I started speaking he took blood samples from five people in the audience. When the seminar ended four hours later, he again took blood samples from those five people. The endorphin and cortisol levels had increased by 300 percent. Since then Dr. Tennant has conducted additional experiments and has made these fascinating findings:

> There is a biochemical basis for why people feel good after these talks. Something about hearing about success gives us an emotional charge that releases those chemicals into the bloodstream and that makes the body function better. And while these effects last for no more than a few hours, regular doses of motivation will lead to better health, happiness, and achievement.

When your energy and confidence are high, the natural tendency not to call on people of wealth and prestige will gradually diminish until it disappears altogether. Go out and establish the habits that will allow you to maintain the proper attitude for the healthy and successful life you deserve to live!

THE KEY TO OVERCOMING CALL RELUCTANCE

I have saved the most essential tip in overcoming call reluctance for last. What follows comes as close to being a "sure thing" as most salespeople will ever experience.

Before I began my formal sales career, staying on a specific time schedule had not been a problem. But when I began my full-time sales career, I moved fifty miles from anyone else in the company. My only contact with my manager was the Monday morning sales meeting and an infrequent phone call. In essence, *everything* was up to me! I really enjoyed my freedom. *No* set time to go to work, *no* set time to finish, *no* direction in between. The only problem with that was—*no* sales and *no* money! My major problems were those of organization and discipline.

In those initial years I also suffered from a serious self-image problem and took it quite personally when anyone would refuse to allow me to make my presentation. A personal rejection, which is what I interpreted the prospect's resistance to be, meant that I would then have to spend time rethinking my situation and alternating between pouting, meditating, having a "pity party," and planning what to do next. Put all these misperceptions together and you get a terrible combination of procrastination and call reluctance.

How I wish someone had explained to me that when people refused to let me make my presentation or turned down my marvelous offer, they were not rejecting me. In their minds it was a simple *business refusal*. The prospects either had no interest in my offer or did not possess the financial resources to make the purchase. They would have said no to anyone.

At that time I also needed someone to explain the importance of a schedule. After I had been in the world of professional selling for two and a half years, Mr. P. C. Merrell entered my life. Mr. Merrell had developed our sales training programs and had set many of the sales records. He was a marvelous role model. In a nutshell, Mr. Merrell convinced me that I really did have ability and worth. He persuaded me that I could, in fact, be the national champion. He also persuaded me that to realize my potential and stabilize my production, I needed to *believe in myself and get on an organized program followed in a disciplined manner.*

He specifically suggested that regardless of what time I finished my work in the evening, I should make an appointment with myself to call on my first prospect at precisely the same time the next day. He emphasized that it really did not make that much difference (within reasonable limitations) what that time was, but I should follow through on that commitment, despite any other little "obstacles" or "interruptions" that came my way. I recognize that this sounds very simple, but that's exactly what success in life and success in selling is all about—doing the little things that make the big difference. For salespeople who are away from the direct supervision of management, failing to go to work at a regular time on a regular basis is one of the biggest reasons for failure. Organization, discipline, and commitment make for consistent high-volume production.

If you get nothing else out of this chapter (or maybe this book), please hear me on this key point. One of the most important ways to overcome call reluctance is this: *Get on a regular schedule and make an appointment with yourself to contact a prospect at the same time every day!*

Make the appointment with yourself, and when the time comes head for that telephone or that prospect. When I made that adjustment, the sales results were dramatic! There is a simple yet profound psychological reason: *Logic will not change an emotion, but action will!* Call reluctance is an emotion, and it will not be overcome consistently by logic. Get into action, support the action with logic, and sales success is sure to be yours!

5
___

Sell by Design, Not by Chance

Getting in front of a client with a brochure and saying, "Stop me when you see something you like" just won't make it. You can make an occasional sale with this method, but you can't make a living—and you certainly can't build a career.

The current market has "marketing savvy" to a much larger degree than at any time in the history of the world. The dinosaur is extinct, and so are the career hopes of any salesperson wearing a plaid coat who comes across as the back-slapping, fast-talking, joke-telling, high-pressure, have-I-got-a-deal-for-you salesperson.

Today's successful persuader must have a specific plan of action that will transcend product line and situational differences.

The Four-Step Formula

The Ziglar Training System's planned-selling process consists of a four-step formula. The first step is Need Analysis, second is Need Awareness, third is Need Solution, and finally, Need Satisfaction. The time spent on each step may vary, but if you are successful in sales, you will be involved in some form of each of these steps.

STEP ONE: NEED ANALYSIS

Customer-driven (wants) and need-oriented (needs) selling begins with the sales professional doing a Need Analysis. Even if the prospects are coming to you and asking for your product or service, it is entirely possible that they have not properly identified what they are really looking for.

In Need Analysis, the goal is to x-ray the prospect. The sales professional develops the skill and talents necessary to look within the customer and find the needs of the customer—to uncover existing needs. These needs may be on the surface or just below the surface, but they definitely exist. Your duty (and opportunity) as a sales professional is to get those needs out into the open.

As you are searching for needs, "wants" will surface. Don't make the mistake of discounting these wants as frivolous because prospects take action on their "want to's" as well as their needs. For our purposes, *wants* and *needs* are basically used interchangeably.

Needs and Wants—Reasons and Excuses. Today's successful

salesperson is *customer-desire driven and needs-oriented!* People buy because they either *need* or *want* something. If we can give someone a reason for buying *and* an excuse for buying, the chances are rather dramatically improved that he will buy.

For example, the *reasons* people buy home computers and cell phones are (1) they want these high-tech products and (2) other family members and peers have the products. The *excuses* people have for buying them are (1) convenience and (2) communication improvement. Again, each "excuse" is legitimate, but the overwhelming factor in buying is "want to" (which is enhanced by others' ownership).

Experience Speaks. Many years ago, when I was in direct sales selling cookware, I made a presentation to a family that desperately *needed* my cookware. I had the opportunity to inventory their kitchen utensils while preparing the demonstration meal, and they had *nothing*. Because their need was so great, I spent nearly two hours attempting to close the sale. The lady and her husband had the same level of intensity in their ability to persevere as I did because they continued to say, "No money, too expensive, can't afford it!"

As I was packing my sample case to leave, the husband, his wife, or I mentioned "china." To this day I can still remember the way that dear lady's eyes lit up. She said, "China? Do you sell fine china?"

"Yes, ma'am," I responded. "We sell the *finest* fine china in the whole world!"

Less than thirty minutes later, I left that household with an order worth substantially more than the entire set of cookware. Now think with me. If she couldn't afford the set of cookware she so desperately needed, how could she afford the china she didn't need? The answer is, she *couldn't* afford a set of cookware she *didn't want*, but she *could* afford a set of fine china she *did want*.

Here is the key point: *People buy what they want when they want it more than they want the money it costs.*

How do you uncover wants and needs? I'm glad you asked.

Probing. With the proper probing effort, you can discover the needs of the prospect. Each has a bundle of needs and wants. Often these are masked by symptoms. The salesperson who sells to symptoms fails to make sales and does not understand why, or has sales *fall out, come back,* or *returned,* whichever term you might use for losing sales, commissions, and the chance to help a prospect.

You want to ask questions to gather information, not to gather facts. Although you want factual information, facts alone won't help you discover the needs of the prospect. The next two chapters contain details on the right kinds of questions.

STEP TWO: NEED AWARENESS

In the Need Awareness step, there are two distinct parts. In the first place, the salesperson must have identified one or more specific needs that can be clearly articulated. In the second place, the prospect must understand that there is a need AND the specifics of the need. The "lightbulb" must first come on in your mind and then in the prospect's mind.

Tuff Stuff. You get started in Need Awareness in the same way you began Need Analysis—by asking questions. But Need Awareness is difficult because to ask questions that cause both you and the prospect to understand the needs and wants, you are required to *think!* Now the reason this is difficult is that "us sales folks" are often so intent on getting the sale that we stop thinking—or we think about the result we want to the detriment of the process we must go through to achieve that result.

Even if prospects are coming to you in a retail environment, and especially when they are not coming to you, developing Need Awareness is vital. I know some of you will find this hard to believe, but some prospects will actually tell you that they want to buy and then change their minds! (Yes, that lump in my cheek is my tongue.) If you have not identified the proper need *and* made that need perfectly clear to the prospect, either the sale will not be made, or it will not stick.

STEP THREE: NEED SOLUTION

Step three in the four-step formula that fits all sales products and services is Need Solution. In this step you present your product. Now is the time to stop asking questions and begin presenting solutions to needs.

Remember: You do not *invent* or *create* the needs. That's not selling. You uncover a need or problem that is already there and, in the process, render a solution, a real service.

You have spent two phases of the professional sales process discovering and tuning in to needs and wants, so don't lead with your product at this point. Let me explain by asking you a series of *trick* questions. Now, I did say they were designed to be misleading, so consider yourself warned. Have you ever purchased a bed? A new outfit? An automobile? An insurance policy? A copier for the office? A training program? A set of audiotapes? A book?

Let me submit to you that not one of you reading this book has ever bought any of these items. What you bought was a good night's sleep; the way you look and feel in a particular outfit; transportation; protection for your family with savings and investment advantages; increased communication and organization for the office; added productivity; more information; a fundamental sales program that will help you be even more successful in your sales career.

None of us buy products. We all buy products of the

product—which are called benefits or need solutions. In short, we don't buy what the product is; we buy what the product *does for us.*

Lead with Need. We never lead with product; we lead with need. Everyone listens to the same radio station according to my friend and fellow sales trainer Don Hutson. Don says, and I agree completely, that every one of us listens to radio station WII-FM—and those call letters stand for *What's In It For Me?* We must relate to the prospect in terms of need, not in terms of product.

Communication consultant Nick Dalley has done some contract work for our organization. It had been several months since any of us had seen him, and several people noticed that there was something different about Nick when he returned to help us with a particular project. We eventually realized he was wearing braces on his teeth. Finally, someone's curiosity led him to ask Nick why he wanted braces.

Nick's answer contains a valuable lesson about WII-FM and leading with need. He responded, "I don't want braces. I want straight teeth."

Please don't waste your time and the prospect's time telling them what the product IS. Tell them what it can DO and why it will do it for them. In Chapter 9 you will learn how to tell people what you are selling, what it does, and why it will do what it does for them better than anything else!

STEP FOUR: NEED SATISFACTION

The fourth step in the process is Need Satisfaction. Here is the most important step the salesperson can take when it comes to helping others. If you truly have a desire to help other people; if you truly believe in your product or service; if you truly want the prospect to benefit; if you truly want to benefit financially from your hard work and effort; then you must remember:

A.A.F.T.O.: Always Ask For The Order. As silly as this may seem to some of you, we sometimes freeze up, burn out, or just "blow it" when the time for the close is near. This is such a common mistake that I wrote an entire book called *Secrets of Closing the Sale.* It has sold hundreds of thousands of copies because we all want to close more sales more often. In Chapter 10 you will learn how to ask for and get the order.

6

QUESTIONS ARE THE ANSWER—
NEED ANALYSIS

What is the best way to begin the sales presentation? With questions! What is the purpose of beginning with questions? Questions allow us to gather important information, which enables us to help our clients, *and* just as important (maybe more important), when we ask questions in a professional manner we establish the most important aspect of the sales process—*trust!*

ASK YOURSELF

If you were to ask me a series of questions in a professional manner that showed a *sincere* interest in me and my company, what would I think of you? If you handle this portion of the sales presentation in the proper manner, I would learn that you are not "just another salesperson out to separate me from my money." Instead, I would discover that you are truly interested in helping me!

Questions are important, but a series of obvious questions designed to lead the prospects "through the hoops" and manipulate them to the point of reaching into "deep pockets" to dig out their hard-earned dollars for you or me is not unlike a root canal without Novocain—it will not be tolerated! As professionals, we need to "motivate" the prospects to share their needs, wants, problems, and interests with us so we can "motivate" them to use our services to solve their problem.

This brings us to an ethical question, and ethics is the foundation upon which we must build a career. What is the difference between motivation and manipulation? Unfortunately, these terms are often confused, but comparing motivation to manipulation is like comparing kindness to deceit. The difference lies in the intent of the person. Motivation will cause people to act out of free choice and desire while manipulation often results in forced compliance. One is ethical and longlasting, and the other is unethical and temporary.

THINKING VS. FEELING QUESTIONS

When you ask questions to discover how the customer feels, you are far more likely to find out what the person thinks. Most of us claim to make logical decisions, but the reality is, we generally make emotional decisions.

However, as salespeople we must understand that if we use

only emotion-creating questions, we might well get the prospects to take action, but what happens when the emotion of the moment fades? "Buyer's remorse" may set in, and we can lose sales that appeared very solid at the moment of closure. On the other hand, if we use only logical questions (which the prospects answer out of their intellect), we might well educate them about their needs and the benefits of our product or service, but there is a strong likelihood that they will go down the street and buy from someone who gets them emotionally involved in the benefits of the product. Therefore, it behooves us to combine emotion and logic. Emotion makes the prospects take action now, and logic enables them to justify the purchase later.

Combining Emotion and Logic

Let's presume you have a product or service that saves your prospect money. At the end of your demonstration or presentation, when you have conclusively shown that your product or service does indeed save the prospect money, you should ask three questions:

"Can you see where our product would save you money?"

"Are you interested in saving money?"

"If you were ever going to start saving money, when do you think would be the best time to start?"

One of the strongest emotions we face is FEAR. And you probably have heard the old sales adage, "Fear of loss is greater than the desire for gain." Obviously, you are trying to help the prospect by taking away the fear of losing money. (You didn't create the fear; you are helping to eliminate it.) Your first question—"Can you see where our product would save you money?"—begins the "fear elimination" process. You are now speaking to your prospect on an *emotional* level.

The second question may seem quite obvious, but it must be asked. This direct question—"Are you interested in saving money?"—brings the prospect from the world of emotion into the world of *logic*. "Of course, I'm interested in saving money; any sensible person is interested in saving money" would be the mental response, even if the oral response is simply yes.

Now, by the prospect's own admission, your product saves money, and the person is adamant in the desire to save money. Question three—"If you were ever going to start saving money, when do you feel would be the best time to start?"—calls for immediate action! It also is a reminder (emotionally) that failure to take action might result in further losses of money.

If your product or service has a health benefit, you may use this same three-question process. In the areas of exercise equipment, vitamins, health club memberships, or physical therapy, the questions might be:

"Can you see where this could be beneficial to your health?"

"Are you seriously interested in maintaining (or regaining) good, vibrant health?"

"Under these circumstances, when do you think it would be best to start really taking care of the health that you obviously cherish so highly?"

Let me challenge you to stop here and determine the number one benefit of the product or service you are involved in selling. What is the primary reason you might move people to take action on your product or service? Now develop your personalized version of the three questions that tie emotion to logic.

My primary benefit (what my product or service does for others) is: _____

My "customized" three questions are:

"Can you see _____?"

"Are you interested in _____?"

"When do you think _____?"

If you didn't take the time to write out these questions, may I ask you a few questions? Can you see where tying emotion to logic in the sales process would help you to close more sales? Are you interested in closing more sales? When do you think would be the best time to begin closing more sales?

THE PROPER QUESTIONING PROCESS

Three basic types of questions allow us to discover the needs and wants of our clients and potential customers. And all questions—emotional or logical—fall into one of these three categories.

OPEN-DOOR QUESTIONS

The first is the Open-Door Question. Open-Door Questions allow the persons being questioned to go wherever they like with their responses. After all, your purpose is not to close in the prospects—you want them to move freely in the areas of their choosing. Open-Door Questions are identified as the "who, what, where, when, how, and why" questions. They may also begin with the phrases "What do you think about . . . ?" or "How do you feel about . . . ?"

Examples of Open-Door Questions are:

1. What is the most exciting aspect of your job?

2. How do you see your responsibilities changing in the next five years?

Again, the purpose of the Open-Door Question is to allow the prospects the freedom to take the answer where they want it to go. If you ask questions that have only yes or no answers, you allow the prospects to remain noncommittal and noninformational. Ask Open-Door Questions.

A Pet Peeve. A major error in asking Open-Door Questions is supplying answers. You are not giving a multiple-choice test! When you ask Open-Door Questions, there will often be a moment of silence. Although that can be terribly uncomfortable, a pause is often necessary for the person to form an insightful and intelligent response to your question. Please avoid offering answers to the question based on your discomfort or the desire to show your insights into the situation.

CLOSED-DOOR QUESTIONS

The second kind of question is the Closed-Door Question. If an Open-Door Question is designed to allow the prospects to move freely wherever their thoughts take them, then the Closed-Door Question is designed to keep them in a certain area for clarification or embellishment. Closed-Door Questions begin with phrases like "Would you tell me more about . . . ?" or "That's fascinating. What do you mean by . . . ?"

Some samples of Closed-Door Questions are:

1. How does your division compare in size to the other divisions in this company?

2. Since your goal is to increase profits, how would the company use those additional profits?

YES OR NO QUESTIONS

The third type of question is the Yes or No Question. This question demands a direct response. However, we will use this question only when we already know the answer. The danger of this kind of question is that if it is overused, it may be perceived as patronizing.

As we construct simple Yes or No Questions, remember to

put them in your own words and the framework of your own personality.

1. Do you agree that this would save you money?

2. Would what I'm proposing fit into your goals?

Yes or No Questions allow you to "test the waters" and check on your progress in the sales process. Some trainers call these questions "trial closes" because they can tell you if you are getting "buy-in" from the prospect based on the response.

YOUR MOST NEGLECTED SALES TOOL

Without reservation, one of the most important (and the least developed) sales tools is the salesperson's voice. Most speech therapists agree that only 5 percent of the people in our society have naturally pleasant voices. Virtually all the rest, however, can be trained. How? Even as you read these words, I encourage you to get in a room by yourself and *not only* read these words out loud but record them as well. Remember to ask this question while listening to yourself on tape: "Would I buy from this person?"

Let me encourage you to tape record the questions you will ask hundreds of times, and if you are the true sales professional

I believe you are, you will take the "extra step" and practice using the proper voice inflection for the answers and objections you deal with on a regular basis. By using a cassette recorder to practice your responses to client statements, you are training your voice and honing your persuasion skills, both critical steps to becoming the consummate professional.

INTERVIEW OR INTERROGATION?

While I hope this next statement is obvious, let me share with you that it is vital for you to *use your own words and work within the framework of your own personality*. Your job is to interview, explore, and uncover customer wants and needs like a caring counselor, not like a prosecuting attorney.

Are you showing a sincere interest in the prospect? Are the questions based on what is being discussed (previous answers), or are you just going down your prepared list? The only thing more frustrating than the poor talk-show host who asks questions regardless of the answer to the previous question is the nonprofessional salesperson who does the same thing.

7

CONDUCTING THE
COMFORTABLE INTERVIEW

My friend and fellow speaker Jim Cathcart teaches a seminar on the "inner" view. Isn't the name terrific? Just thinking of doing an "innerview" instead of an interview will help paint the kind of picture in your mind that is necessary to be successful in gathering information in the Need Analysis segment of the sales process. If you will make conducting an "innerview" (with your prospect) your goal, your sales career will be greatly enhanced!

THE P.O.G.O. FORMULA

Even some very successful sales professionals have difficulty "firing" off a series of questions to a prospect they are meeting for the first time. Still others struggle with asking for information without giving some first.

The P.O.G.O. formula will allow you to get involved in a conversational interview process that will be comfortable for you *and* the prospect. P.O.G.O. gives you a track to run on and specific direction on how to best meet the "comfort-level" needs of the prospect.

PERSON

The *P* in the P.O.G.O. formula stands for *Person. Anything* that expresses a *sincere* interest in the prospect will be valuable to you. I encourage you to design a series of questions right now that relate to the person. Remember that it is okay to share some personal information about yourself, but *you* already know about you. Give just enough about yourself to express common interests but not enough to monopolize the conversation. Limit personal revelations to 25 percent of this part of the conversation. In other words, three parts prospect to one part salesperson.

The true professional, who really cares about prospects and clients, also gathers information for follow-up visits and calls. Casually asking how the big game turned out or where the prospect and the spouse decided to have their anniversary dinner can go a long way toward letting others know that you really do care about them and will treat them as the very important people they truly are. The key words to remember in the process are *brief, warm, sincere,* and *friendly.*

Developing People Questions. My friend Gerhard Gschwandtner, the publisher of *Selling Power* magazine, has a wonderful workbook called *The Sales Question Book*, which contains hundreds of sample questions arranged in specific categories. Get a copy of Gerhard's manual and take the time to adapt these questions to meet your situation and make the questions your own.

Samples of people-focused questions are below.

Open-Door Questions—Person

1. How did you get into this particular business?

2. What part of the country do you come from originally?

Closed-Door Questions—Person

1. How long have you been a (golfer, tennis enthusiast, hunter)?

2. Other than working here, what type career experiences have you pursued?

Yes or No Questions—Person

1. Do you like living in Dallas?

2. Are you able to spend significant time with your family?

ORGANIZATION

The first *O* in the P.O.G.O. formula stands for *Organization*. As the conversation about the person draws to a close, move to the organization. Again, probe gently, and be willing to talk about your organization. But the same rule applies as in the "person" aspect of P.O.G.O.—25 percent about your organization to 75 percent about the prospect's.

I am *not* saying you cannot talk about your company. Some prospects are very interested to know about you, and you need to give them enough information to build confidence that your company is solid and reputable. However, do not monopolize the conversation. Your objective is to give them enough information to build that confidence . . . and to gather enough information to make you effective (i.e., make the sale).

Developing Organizational Questions. Here are some sample questions that might be adaptable for you.

Open-Door Questions—Organization

1. Would you tell me something about your organization?

2. What part of your operation interests you and creates the most excitement in the business community?

Closed-Door Questions—Organization

1. How is the _____ department performing?

2. What kind of training is the leadership of your organization receiving?

Yes or No Questions—Organization

1. Are you satisfied with your bottom-line profits?

2. Is your organization growing at the rate you desire?

Goals

The *G* in the P.O.G.O. formula stands for *Goals*. This is the time for gathering information about personal and professional goals. Many nonprofessionals are so pleased to get a response that they hurry along to the next part of the process. The true professional will continue to probe.

Questions for Discovering Goals. Following are some sample questions that you might adapt for your goal "innerview."

Open-Door Questions—Goals

1. What are your personal/organizational goals?

2. How did you determine these were top-priority goals?

Closed-Door Questions—Goals

1. How are you currently tracking the progress of your goals?

2. What is your time frame to achieve your goal?

Yes or No Questions—Goals

1. Have your goals been realistic in the past?

2. You are using an established goal-setting process, aren't you?

Unachieved Goals. Why do so few people actually achieve their goals? Primarily because they have never really identified the true goals.

Many times a prospect's goals will involve money. I want to submit to you that money is never a goal! The real goal revolves around *what can be done* with the money. Whether it's to build a monument to themselves (a beautiful home) or build a wing onto an orphanage, it is most important that the real goal be identified.

When you ask a prospect about goals and you get a money response, and you follow with, "Why would that be important to you?" you are beginning to discover true goals. Many will have given their goals very little thought. While this portion of the selling process must not digress into a counseling session, your goal must be for the prospect to "get real" with you. Many sales "blow up" on even experienced sales professionals because they did not probe for the real goals.

OBSTACLES

The second *O* in the P.O.G.O. formula stands for *Obstacles* to reaching the goals just discussed. As Dr. Norman Vincent Peale said, "If you want to meet someone who has no problems, no obstacles in life, just go down to the cemetery . . . and come to think about it, some of them have a tremendous problem."

Everyone with whom we come in contact has problems. I once heard a man state, "You go up to anyone on the street and say, 'I heard about your problem,' and the person will ask, 'Who told you?'" Problems are the mutual ground you share with your client. But the key doesn't lie in not having problems; the key lies in finding solutions to those problems.

Questions for Discovering Obstacles. The following are sample questions to help you discover obstacles.

Open-Door Questions—Obstacles

1. What is preventing you from being where you want to be?

2. What are the obstacles you are facing?

Closed-Door Questions—Obstacles

1. What are you doing to overcome _____
   (a specific obstacle)?

2. Which obstacle is the most crucial to overcome?

Yes or No Questions—Obstacles

1. Do you feel there are other steps you might take
   in overcoming obstacles?

2. Have you designed a plan to overcome the
   obstacles that seem to be holding you back?

PREPARATION

The P.O.G.O. Formula is one great tool for preparation. It is impossible to be "too prepared" for a sales presentation. When you are thoroughly prepared, the left brain (the carefully directed, organized, logical, and concretely sequential lobe of the brain) is already functioning at maximum capacity. This allows your right brain (the creative, freewheeling, visual lobe of the brain) to handle the interruption or distraction in the most effective manner possible. Preparation is vital to success.

Early in your sales career, you may need to "struggle" through some of these tough learning processes. Preparation helps enormously.

How Much Time? An integral part of preparation is time allocation. When you are involved in the P.O.G.O. process, you should have a solid feel for how much time you will be allowed to spend with the prospect. Once you commit to a length of time, be sure to exceed that time *only at the request of the prospect.*

Some prospects are incredibly impatient, even showing their impatience as early as Need Analysis. They are driven and impetuous and want "just the facts" without any "window dressing" along the way. When the prospect demands to know "what it will do for me and how much it will cost," you need to move immediately into benefit selling. Emphasize your most dramatic point—the reason the largest number of people buy your product or service—by asking a question. When you get a positive, responsive answer (and you will more often than not), simply say, "Then let me get right to the point . . ." and continue your planned professional presentation.

There is no need for you to get off track or panic or begin closing immediately. Stay with your plan and do an *abbreviated* version of each step. But if you are giving your shortened sales talk and the prospect continues to interrupt, stop and say, "Mr. Prospect, I really want to serve you in the best manner possible. Would it be better if we rescheduled this meeting for another time?" If the prospect says yes, set an appointment and leave immediately. As soon as possible, meet with your sales manager to evaluate the call. Some people must get to the bottom line more quickly than others, and some salespeople labor the presentation. Let your sales manager help you determine the cause in this situation.

Many times the prospect will ask "I'm ready to buy" questions: How many sizes do you offer in this product? Is this the only color? Do you have a payment plan? When this occurs ask the closing question, "Which size and color would meet your needs best?" When he answers—write the order. (Don't insist on finishing your presentation.)

MOVING INTO NEED AWARENESS

And now is the moment of truth. Now that you know the Person, the Organization, the Goals, and the Obstacles to those goals, what do you do? You begin the next step in the sales process—Need Awareness.

8

MAKING THE LIGHTS GO ON— NEED AWARENESS

Even when you are sure you have discovered the client's need, you must continue to probe for two basic reasons: (1) to be sure you have the true need and not a symptom of the need; and (2) to be sure the prospect understands that there really is a need.

HOMEOSTATIC BALANCE

Bryan Flanagan introduced me to the term *homeostatic balance* several years ago. The natural law of homeostasis says that an organism stays in perfect balance until acted upon by an outside force. The outside force causes the status quo to be disrupted, and the organism becomes out of balance. We rarely take *action* until we are out of balance. Once we are out of balance, we will take the proper steps to correct or right our balance.

Homeostatic balance is helping the prospect understand there is a need (turning on the light for the prospect). And by showing where the prospect is out of balance, the sales professional upsets the homeostatic balance.

Unbalanced Prospects

I am *not* advocating that you knock the prospect off balance. You must discover where an imbalance already exists and point it out in a convincing manner. In essence, this makes your prospect uncomfortable or unhappy with his condition or situation, which means you are now in position to make a sale because your prospect wants to solve his problem.

When the prospect becomes aware of his imbalance, three things can happen. First, the salesperson makes the sale and now has to worry about how to spend the commissions. Second, the prospect discovers his imbalance, but the salesperson doesn't ask for the order. Then, over a period of time the prospect regains balance and forgets he was ever uncomfortable. Third, the prospect discovers he is out of balance, the salesperson doesn't ask for the order, and the competition comes in and asks for the order, rights the prospect, and makes the sale. Then everyone is happy—but you!

Training for Need Awareness

To help the prospect discover his area of imbalance, you must ask questions. Those questions will be based on your knowledge of your product, industry, pricing, application, and competition.

1. PRODUCT KNOWLEDGE

Enthusiasm for the product or service comes from product knowledge and talking with satisfied customers. How can we develop enthusiasm for something about which we have little or no knowledge? Get information on the history of the product, how it is made or manufactured, and how it does what it does and why. You will want to constantly study the product and any improvements made to it.

2. INDUSTRY KNOWLEDGE

The more you know about your industry in general, the more you are able to understand the all-important "why." Again, go back to the history of your industry. Understand how the group of products or services evolved to their current level. Then go beyond history to industry analysis. Where is your industry going over the next five to ten years? What are the future trends that would help you to help more people?

Every industry has several trade publications filled with feature articles, trend analysis charts, the latest information on legal matters, ideas on advertising, and news about people in the industry. Your effectiveness in your next sales call might well depend on your basic industry knowledge, and in-depth customer profiles will set you apart from the vast majority of people in the sales profession.

3. PRICING KNOWLEDGE

Why does your product or service require the investment that you are asking from a prospect? How can you justify asking that amount of money for that number of benefits? What are your profit margins? Do you understand the difference between cost and price?

Pricing knowledge includes many different areas: maximizing profits in difficult markets, proper pricing for the market, adapting pricing strategy to the changing economy, and negotiating prices. However, most of us in sales will not deal with these areas. We need to focus on showing the prospects how and why the price of our product or service is fair to them.

Many salespeople erroneously believe that price is the determining factor in most sales. I'm convinced that in most sales the exact opposite is true.

Bill Callaway, from Farmington, Missouri, shared my belief when he was a salesman for an office supply company in Flat River, Missouri, that sold personal computers. He called on a nursing home and was told that the owners would have to discuss his proposal. In other words, they wanted to "think about it." Despite his best efforts, he could not close the sale because they really did need time to discuss his proposal. A week later, he got the bad news that the nursing home owners had checked out a similar computer system in St. Louis, which was made by the same manufacturer and was $1,600 cheaper, so they were quite naturally interested in the less expensive model.

Bill decided he was not going to take no for an answer but would help them get what *they* really *wanted* and *needed*.

Bill used the following approach: "Considering your needs now and in the future, how long do you feel would be a reasonable life span for the computer you choose?" The buyer responded, "At least ten years."

"The difference," Bill continued, "between the computer I offer and the one you looked at in St. Louis is approximately $1,600. So let's look at what the difference means over the ten years you agreed would be an acceptable life span. Actually, that's only $160 a year, or about $13 a month, which is roughly $0.43 a day." Then Bill asked the big question: "Would it be worth an extra $0.43 per day to do business with a company that you have repeatedly agreed would offer you the proper training and service that are so important to you?"

"Yes, it would!" was the response, and Bill was ecstatic!

Bill didn't spill all his information in the initial stages of the presentation. He saved additional points to use when asking for the order.

Since the fear of loss is often greater than the desire for

gain, Bill might have asked, "Is $0.43 a reasonable price to pay for peace of mind?" or "Have you ever calculated what it would cost you to be without this computer if proper service were not available for even one day, much less a week or longer?" The fear of not having the computer, which is a real fear, would be of paramount concern to the customer. In this case, the manufacturer was the same, and the physical equipment was almost the same. The BIG difference was the salesperson and the service he could offer.

Major Point: Never, never, never forget that price involves a great deal more than money!

4. APPLICATION KNOWLEDGE

The use or application of your product will help you enormously in showing the prospect the need for your product. Implementation is vital to usage, and usage is vital to "word-of-mouth" marketing, which can aid you tremendously. If you understand how your product, goods, or services can be used, *and* you can help others understand the process, you will help more people and make more sales.

5. COMPETITION KNOWLEDGE

When you fail to make the sale, do you know why? In most cases, you are up against an "outside" competitor. Do you know with whom you compete? Do you know why you are beating them? Do you know why you lose sales to them? Your knowledge of your competitors will help you in many ways when you are showing the prospects how you can meet their needs. In our information age, take full advantage of technology to stay ahead of the competition.

DISCOVERING AREAS OF IMBALANCE

If you have prepared yourself with knowledge, then you can move on to the questions. The most important thing to remember when showing the imbalance to the prospect is to be sure that you have a solution. What could be more frustrating than discovering a serious problem with no solution? Are you in this business to help or hurt people? If you make a sale that solves a problem (corrects an imbalance) and you are rewarded, don't you *and* the prospect win? If you don't have the prospect's best interests at heart, shouldn't you find something else to do?

ARE ALL THE LIGHTS ON?

Once the light goes on for you (you know the prospect's need and know you have the solution) and the light goes on for the prospect (the person knows that there is a need and that you have a solution), you must move to the Need Solution segment of the sales process.

9

SELLING TO PEOPLE'S PROBLEMS— NEED SOLUTION

J. Kevin Jenkins of Lafayette, Louisiana, sold proper pelvic tilt, blood flow, relaxed muscles, peace of mind, lack of stress, and a rested and relaxed mind and body.

Kevin began his presentation with scientific validation from chiropractors and medical doctors substantiating factual information that showed how using his product for an extended period enhances health and well-being. Next, he brought in customer testimonials and showed how using his product could save the prospect two hours—when comparisons were made to his competition. Everything he talked about with his prospects translated into a customer benefit, which is, after all, the only reason anybody buys anything from anybody.

By now some of you have realized that Kevin sold water beds, but may I ask you a question? If you could be shown how you might receive all those benefits, would you care what the product was? By painting a compelling picture of free time and health benefits while using simple arithmetic, Kevin Jenkins was winning *and* helping others to win.

Personalize the benefits for the prospect. Paint the person into the picture driving that luxury car, receiving compliments on the beautiful dress or suit, looking at the sunset on the lake where the new home has been constructed, or sitting in the comfortable retirement environment provided by the investment being made. Paint the picture so your prospect *sees* personal benefits.

TWO VITAL QUESTIONS

When we provide solutions, we do not sell products. People do not buy products. They buy products of the products—known as *benefits*.

Let me challenge you right now to stop and answer what should be two simple questions. There may be as many as three answers to each question, but please answer these as completely as possible.

The first question: What do you sell?

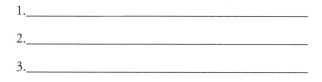

1._____

2._____

3._____

The second question: What do your prospects buy?

1._____

2._____

3._____

And now if you will allow me a third question, it will be this: Do those lists match? If the answer is yes, you are miles ahead of many of your competitors. If you did not stop to think about your answers, let me encourage you to take the time to give these seemingly simple questions your sincere effort. The answers will reveal a great deal about you. Those who refuse to take the time to answer these questions and minimize their importance are most often those who don't have a clue about the answers.

MY ANSWERS

Allow me to answer the two questions I asked you to answer. The first question: What do you sell? I sell life-changing tools that empower people to overcome negative patterns of the past and make progress in the present while having hope in the future. The second question: What do your prospects buy? People purchase tools that give them power over their past, progress in the present, and hope in the future. And yes, these two match.

Feature—Function—Benefit

In the great profession of selling there is much talk about features, functions, and benefits, but what are these wonderful items? In order to "lead with need" we must have an understanding of the basic definitions of these key words.

A *feature* is a part of the product or service—or what the product or service *is*. There may be several features per product or service. A ballpoint pen has a clip; this is a feature.

A *function* is the act that particular part of the product or service performs—or what that particular part of the product or service *does*. There may be several functions per product or service. The clip of the ballpoint pen functions to hold the pen to your pocket.

A *benefit* is the *advantage* in using the feature and the function—or what the feature and function *do for the prospect/client*. There may be many benefits per product or service. The clip of the ballpoint pen saves you money and frustration because you don't lose it or keep misplacing it.

The Classic Example

Those who train *feature, function,* and *benefit* often use the ballpoint pen as the classic example. However, the classic example for you is your product or service. Would you stop right now and list at least three features, three functions, and three benefits of what you are selling?

Features

_____

_____

_____

Functions

_____

_____

_____

Benefits

_____

_____

_____

When providing a solution to a prospect's need (solving a problem), you always lead with the need. There will be times when you will reference features and functions—this information will convince the prospect that you know your business and understand the value of your product. However, the prospect won't give you any money until you've clearly spelled out the benefits.

Salespeople need to clearly understand that prospects do not buy what the product is; they buy the benefits that the use of the product will bring to them. "Antilock brakes" mean very little to the average driver until you explain that they may prevent those dangerous skids on slippery highways. Five inches of insulation mean nothing until you translate them into lower heating and air-conditioning costs.

Now that you thoroughly understand the importance of leading with need, and the difference in features, functions, and benefits, you are ready to Always Ask For The Order— A.A.F.T.O.

10

THE ABC's OF CLOSING SALES—
NEED SATISFACTION

Many years ago, the Detroit newspapers carried a feature story about a monstrous insurance policy purchased by Henry Ford. A close friend of Mr. Ford who was in the insurance business was considerably upset and asked him why on earth he had not bought the policy from him. Mr. Ford's answer is a lesson to everybody who sells anything to anybody at any time under any circumstances—and that's all of us! He said, "You didn't ask me."

NEED SATISFACTION

The fourth step in our successful sales formula is Need Satisfaction. Remember, as a persuader, in most cases the prospect really does want to say yes, particularly if you have successfully completed Need Analysis, Need Awareness, and Need Solution, and if you are pleasant, professional, and at least reasonably friendly. We all really do not like to say no because that could possibly end the relationship. The odds are in the professional salesperson's favor, so ask for the order, my selling friend. Do it pleasantly and professionally, but ASK!

We Must "Ask" to "Have"

Sales authority Chris Hegarty reports that 63 percent of all sales interviews end with the salesperson not specifically asking for the order. We must "ask" to "have." Dozens of books are published on the art and science of professional selling each year. However, very few of these books deal exclusively with the closing process. This is one of the reasons my book *Secrets of Closing the Sale* has been so popular and is still the only pure sales-technique book to ever make the *New York Times* Bestseller list.

Persistence and Persuasion

John Cummings of Mundelein, Illinois, understood one of the secrets to closing a sale. When he was the general manager at an automobile dealership, one of John's trainees tried unsuccessfully to get a client to purchase an "experienced" vehicle.

The manager for the area was also unsuccessful in closing the sale. Since between the two of them they had asked the closing question at least four times, the outlook for closing the sale seemed remote. And then the trainee, Jim Borgman, had an idea. About an hour after the prospect had gotten home, Jim called him and greeted him quite cordially, saying, "Mr. Prospect, Jim Borgman from Bernard Chevrolet. Did I take you away from anything important?" After finding out he was calling at a convenient time (which was a wise move), he continued, "I wanted to ask you a couple of questions, may I?" Upon receiving permission to continue, Jim asked, "Did you visit our competition?" The prospect responded, "Why, yes, I did." Jim got directly to the point and asked, "Did you purchase?" "No" was the prospect's one-word reply. "Pretty expensive over there, aren't they?" said Jim. "Yes, they are."

"Mr. Prospect, do you mind if I ask you just one more question?" "No," the prospect responded. "Super!" Jim said enthusiastically. "Mr. Prospect, where are you going to take your first trip in your Suburban from Bernard Chevrolet?" After a slight pause the prospect replied, "Kentucky!" And with a huge smile on his face (that says a prospect and a salesman just experienced the "double win") Jim continued, "Fine, fine, Mr. Prospect. Come on back. I'm sure we can arrive at a fair trading difference." "I'm on my way, Jim."

Initially, Jim and the prospect were $1,500 away from making a deal, but due to the sales rookie's enthusiastic, creative, courteous, and persistent approach—combined with his understanding of the prospect, getting the prospect emotionally involved, and *asking for the order one more time*—Jim Borgman made the sale. Remember: A growing "green" salesperson will sell more than an experienced "blue" one.

Asking for the order five times or more can be extremely difficult if you (a) don't have a deep belief in the value of your product or service; (b) haven't done the proper job with the first three steps (Need Analysis, Need Awareness, and Need Solution) in our four-step selling formula; or (c) don't expect to make the sale. When you persist pleasantly and professionally, you will create a win-win situation.

ASKING AND RECEIVING

K.I.S.S.—*Keep It Simple Salesman*—has been the battle cry since the cave dwellers sold each other "fire sticks." Yes, you may well know more than the one hundred closes included in my book *Secrets of Closing the Sale,* but do you know them well enough to use them at a moment's notice in the proper sales environment?

The key is this: Don't reinvent the wheel. Go to school on other people's experience. Focus on a handful of closes that work for you, such as the Summary Close.

The Summary Close may seem very basic to some of you, but don't minimize the significance of what may seem obvious. In the Summary Close, you recap the areas of the presentation that caused your prospect's eyes to light up—that turned the lightbulb on—and then ask for the order.

During the selling process, the prospects light a fire for themselves based on your providing the starter fluid and the matches. During the selling process, the fire will sometimes die down due to any number of circumstances or distractions. By summarizing what caused the fire to burn brightly, you rekindle the flame at the moment you are asking the prospects to make their investment. The more "feeling" they have at this moment, the more sales you will close.

WHAT IF THEY SAY NO?

When your prospects say no, the reason is most often that they do not "know" enough to say yes. Chapter 11 will help you overcome "no" by placing prospects in the "know."

11

CLOSING MORE SALES MORE OFTEN

This may surprise some of you, but once your prospects say no, they are not going to change their minds and buy from you. Sales veterans will often tell you that the majority of their sales are made after prospects say no, and some statistics say that about 60 percent of sales occur after the prospect has said no five times. However, I stand by my statement that your prospects are not going to "change their minds" and buy from you.

Your prospects, however, will make a *new decision based on new information*. You see, when prospects say no, the successful sales professional understands that the "no" must mean the prospects don't "know" enough to make the "yes" decision. Never argue with them. Just understand that you haven't finished your job, and accept the responsibility for providing the information needed. You must give additional reasons, features, functions, and benefits for the prospect to make the "yes" decision *today*. With additional information, they will "know" enough to make a new (and favorable) decision.

MOVING FROM "NO" TO "KNOW"

To move the prospect from "no" to "know," the successful sales professional asks questions to understand and identify the objection. Next, the salesperson empathizes—that is, understands how the prospect feels without having the same feelings—about the objection. But some prospects will not *tell* you the true objection, and some prospects will not *know* the true objection. In both cases, they are often operating on a "feeling" level. With this in mind, the salesperson must test the objection.

GORILLA DUST

The sales professional recognizes false objections as "gorilla dust." You may have seen the PBS television series showing the behaviors and habits of wild gorillas. When two males engage in battle, they create quite a show. They circle each other several times and rake their hands in the dirt, scooping up handfuls and throwing it in the air, which makes quite a dust storm or smoke screen. This is "gorilla dust," and many prospects will often go through a similar process.

Some of you have heard the old joke about the fellow who refused to loan his lawn mower to his next-door neighbor. When pressed for a reason, he replied, "Because all planes are leaving late today."

"What kind of reason is that?" was his neighbor's indignant response.

"Not much of one, but when you don't want to do something, and you're not gonna do something, one reason is about as good as another," said the fellow.

For the professional sales representative, one reason is *not* as good as another, so to discover true objections, you will want to test.

Two Tests

Two kinds of tests will help you identify the difference between "gorilla dust" and true objections. These tests also help the prospect who really doesn't know what her objection is but knows she can't get comfortable with the decision to buy.

The "Suppose" Test. The first test is the "Suppose" Test, which involves asking the prospect to entertain hypothetical questions:

> "Ms. Prospect, just suppose that condition didn't exist. Would you then invest in my product or service?"

> "Suppose _____ were not a consideration, then would you make a yes decision?"

> "Suppose you felt good about _____, then would you make a yes decision?"

"Suppose _____, then would you make a yes decision?"

If you can identify the proper objection, then you can take steps to overcome it or move on to the next prospect instead of wasting time eliminating "gorilla dust" or trying to close a sale that will never be closed.

The "Isolate and Validate" Test. The second test is the "Isolate and Validate" Test. This two-step process proves whether or not you have discovered the true objection. The first step comes when you ask, "Is there any *other* reason that would prevent you from taking advantage of my offer today?" Your objective here is to draw out any and all objections. One of the most frustrating things that can happen to a salesperson is to deal with an objection competently and professionally and then have another one spring up. After you have answered two objections, you need to specifically ask on the third one, "Is this the only thing standing between you and ownership of our product, or is there something else?" You don't want to give the impression that you are going to be with the prospect all day until he finally comes up with an objection you can't answer.

Once you get the "no, that is the only thing" response, you will summarize to validate. "So, Mr. Prospect, you're telling me that if _____ and _____ were not issues, you would buy today?" When you deal with that final objection you close the sale by asking, "Am I right in believing that you want to start enjoying the benefits as quickly as possible?" That's your close. Write the order.

OBJECTIONS WE ALL SEE

Objections give you insight into the prospects that can help you meet their needs and wants. Whenever possible, objections need to be anticipated. Through your company's training program and your personal experience, you should encounter no more than one or two "new" objections each quarter. There will be the "standards," but not many you will not have heard. Consequently, with careful planning and forethought, you can have reasonable answers ready to present.

After all, objections are part of every sales professional's life. Our attitude toward them makes a tremendous amount of difference in how effective we are going to be in handling objections.

I'LL BE RIGHT BACK

For the famous "I want to think it over" or "Let me think it over for a few days" objection, Tim Jones, from Campbellsville, Kentucky, has discovered a very interesting response. After going through extensive paperwork and data for the prospect, he will ask the obligating question. If the prospect asks for time to "think it over," Tim will smile, stand up and say, "Fine, I'm going to run down to the corner and get a cup of coffee. I'll be back in fifteen to twenty minutes, so you folks go ahead and talk it over." Before the prospect has time for a response he is out the door, leaving the paperwork behind.

Upon returning, Tim resumes where he left off, saying, "Which way did you decide would be best for us to provide this saving to you—monthly, automatic check, or annualized premiums?" More often than not, he gets the sale.

THE GUNFIGHTER

Some salespeople learn to enjoy dealing with objections a little too much. They let their ego enter the picture and may actually encourage objections so that they can demonstrate their intelligence and skill. These salespeople become like gunfighters, hungry for the fight: "Make your move, you dirty prospect. For anything you ask, I have an answer!"

Remember, your objective is not to prove how many objections you can answer but to prove how much your goods and services can benefit the prospect. And the sale does not end when you have overcome objections and the customer says yes. Actually, the sale is just beginning. It ends when the agreement is signed, the goods are serviced, delivered, paid for, and the customer is satisfied.

BEYOND CUSTOMER "SERVICE" TO CUSTOMER "SATISFACTION"

In the "yesteryear" days of selling, an older salesman and a younger salesman were riding the train back home at the end of the week and were involved in a serious conversation. The younger salesman was "singing the blues" about how badly he had been treated all week. Business was bad, people were rude, and he had been insulted time after time. The older salesman grew thoughtful for a moment and then remarked, "Well, you know, I've had doors slammed in my face, I've been invited to leave and encouraged not to come back, I've been fussed at, cussed at, and even spit at, but INSULTED?!?! Never!"

CAN WE "AFFORD" UNHAPPY CUSTOMERS?

All of us can be kind, friendly, and enthusiastic to the people who give us the order, treat us in a friendly manner, and are easy to deal with. My friend, if that's all you're capable of doing, just remember: Your company could hire anybody to deal with those people (and pay considerably less than you're capable of earning). Your value to your company comes basically from the skills you develop in dealing with everybody, including those disgruntled customers and prospects, in an effective and professional manner.

When you encounter a rude, belligerent, unhappy individual, do you in turn react by being rude and belligerent, or do you remember that you have the power of choice? You can choose to respond in a friendly and courteous manner, or you can choose to react in a rude and belligerent manner.

I'll be the first one to admit this is often easier said than done, but stay with me because I want to share ways that will help you make the proper choice more often than not.

Research indicates that roughly 90 percent of our unhappy customers simply stop doing business with us without saying anything at all about it to us. Unfortunately, they do tell friends, relatives, neighbors, and complete strangers. Question: Can we afford unhappy customers?

Take Control Physically—of *You!*

Instead of wringing someone's neck, which is often the first response to the angry person, just relax, force yourself to let your hands hang limply by your sides, and *hear the person out*—don't interrupt! I cannot overemphasize this portion of dealing with the irate person.

Regardless of how angry someone may be, it is difficult to *express* that anger through speech or actions for more than two minutes. If you don't believe me, try it. Get as angry as you want to and shout, scream, rant, rave, whoop, holler, and do anything you like to express your anger/aggravation/irritation. If you will listen until the anger is released, you will have taken much of the steam out of the person with whom you are dealing. *When you interrupt, you allow the person to regain momentum, and the two minutes start over!*

FIND A SOLUTION

When the steam is released, your next strategy is to lower your voice and articulate each word clearly and deliberately. Remember, the person you are dealing with is in a highly charged emotional state. If you relax physically, hear the person out, and then respond in a lower voice, articulating each word clearly, you can bring the individual to your level of calmness. The best way to stay calm is to remove yourself emotionally from the situation. None of this is personal. And if it becomes personal, you need to remove yourself from the situation physically.

You may not agree with that person, and not agreeing is perfectly permissible—if you express yourself properly. Begin the content of your response by thanking the person if it is at all possible. When you calmly respond, "You know, Mr. Prospect, I want to thank you for sharing your honest feelings with me," you haven't compromised yourself or your company. Nor have you agreed that the irate person is correct in thinking and actions. You have let the person know you are going to handle the matter with courtesy.

Continue to assure the person that you are going to help. If you will memorize the following script, you can use it in most situations where you are faced with an angry person.

"Mr. Prospect, thank you for sharing your honest feelings with me. It is important for you to know that I really want to help you. I understand how you feel. You have every right to feel that way. Would you be willing to work with me to find a solution to this uncomfortable situation?"

Remember as you seek a solution to the problem (and not someone to blame) that very few people can get really mad and even fewer can stay that way with an individual who is sincerely trying to solve the problem and resolve the situation.

AFTER THE PROSPECT COOLS DOWN

What happens when the prospects or customers cool down and collect their thoughts? At this point you have a chance to actually increase your business with them. After the confrontation and the resolution, if the customers are completely in the wrong, they will often realize their mistake and become embarrassed. It's critical that you get back to them in a friendly, cheerful, upbeat manner and reiterate how much you appreciate their openness and their willingness to share. Tell them how much you value their business.

This approach will solidify customers. Otherwise, because they've been in the wrong, they might be so embarrassed about their conduct that they will not continue to do business with you. It's the old "extra mile" principle applied again in life and in selling. As sales trainers have said for many years, you must bring the "and then some" principle to life. When you have done everything expected of you as a professional "and then some," you are building an extraordinary sales career.

Abusive Language

Here is another sales presentation that you can memorize or write on an index card to use on those special occasions when someone begins to yell or swear at you:

"Mr. Prospect, when you talk to me like that I feel I can no longer be helpful to you. If you will work with me and focus on the problem, I believe we can come up with a solution. However, if you continue to use profane and abusive language, my integrity demands that I terminate this conversation."

If the abuse continues, do as you have promised. If you are dealing with someone on the phone, allow for a "cooling-off" time and then call back. Chances are excellent that he will be embarrassed by his behavior and will be much easier to work with. Actually, if your spirit is right and you show no anger or vindictiveness, you are in an excellent position to make a sale or solidify the account. Here's why: The prospect or customer feels he did something *to* you; now, he should do something *for* you. That "something" could include an apology, a willingness to listen, and even a desire to "make it right" by buying or continuing to buy from you.

KEY PRINCIPLES

To deal effectively with irate persons, remember the following information.

No one can get "under your skin" and upset you without your permission, so:

- hear them out—let the anger erupt
- be patient
- be tactful
- empathize
- acknowledge their importance
- articulate your response slowly, quietly, and carefully
- never grant them permission to control you

A "SERVICE" FACT OF LIFE

It's a fact of life that if you're going to be in the world of selling very long, there are going to be disagreements and complaints. Look at those disgruntled clients and unhappy prospects as opportunities to grow and become even more successful in your career.

GAINING CONTROL OF YOUR TIME
AND YOUR LIFE

Discipline yourself to do the things you need to do when you need to do them, and the day will come when you will be able to do the things you want to do when you want to do them!

THE TIME OF YOUR LIFE

Authorities estimate that as much as 80 percent of the salesperson's time is involved in activities that do not directly generate business. Many have calculated that less than two hours of the working day are actually spent in the sales process. The rest of the time is spent going from prospect to prospect, waiting in offices, looking for parking spaces, taking care of administrative details, and handling service calls and a host of other things.

The question the sales professional must ask is this: Can I more effectively—or equally effectively—handle this assignment during nonselling hours? I particularly think of answering correspondence, filling out reports, coping with administrative details, obtaining credit reports, and taking care of personal business (seeing the dentist, buying clothing, visiting friends, paying bills, etc.). Successful sales professionals, with no more time than average performers, will spend twice as many hours in front of prospects than average producers do. They make sales not because of exceptional ability but because they have prioritized what's important in what they do on a daily basis.

RECIPE FOR SALES SUCCESS

Generally speaking, the high-producing sales professional does work harder than the average producer. The reality is, simply outworking your competition will put you in the upper echelons of selling. I'm not talking about working eighty- and ninety-hour weeks. One extra hour per day in high-payoff activity will allow you to outdistance most of the field and surprise yourself in terms of people helped and dollars earned. It's a balance of efficiency and effectiveness. "Efficiency" means doing things right; "effectiveness" is doing the right things.

One of the most effective and efficient men I know is Dave Liniger, the founder of Re/Max Realtors. He has established an atmosphere that encourages the people around him to get the most out of their time and themselves.

Dave discovered that 47 percent of the top one hundred Re/Max producers had personal assistants who handled some of the "nonsales" responsibilities. These "helpers" were involved in activities like putting up and taking down "For Sale" and "Sold" signs in yards, making routine phone calls, sending e-mail, dropping mail at the post office, and handling the many details that consume time.

Delegating nonselling tasks frees the professional salesperson to spend more time prospecting for and talking with clients, activities that are far more likely to lead to more sales more often. Increased sales means a boost to the economy and the income of the Re/Max associate. Interestingly enough, while these top producers work longer hours each week than the other sales associates, they are far more likely to take vacations—often taking as much as four weeks off per year.

The conclusion is clear: The better you utilize your time, the more income you will generate; and the more income you generate, the more free time you will have for your family and for taking those really nice trips. In short, higher income salespeople work smarter, not necessarily harder, and they utilize other people more efficiently and effectively so that everybody wins!

What I'm really saying is that the sales career is built before, during, *and* after the sale is made. As we say down home, "Even a blind pig is going to find a good acorn every once in a while." It's also true that even inept salespeople, by the sheer process of making calls, will end up with an occasional sale. But I can guarantee you they won't build a rewarding sales career on that type of hit-or-miss approach.

SELF-ANALYSIS

Many salespeople I've talked with are dissatisfied with their productivity. They know that many of the things they do and the procedures they follow are habitual and are probably no longer effective, perhaps unnecessary, and possibly even harmful. This is why "self-analysis" is so important.

"Self-analysis" is a magnificent procedure that documents your activities and involves regularly asking yourself some questions: "Do I need to perform this activity, or do I need to do it in another way? Can I increase my overall productivity by increasing my effectiveness? Do I really need to work this hard?"

Activity Log. One of the most meaningful activities I have ever been involved with was doing a time analysis chart. I will admit that when I first heard about tracking my time, I felt like I had just been given a prison sentence. Most of us feel we are not being trusted when someone asks us to account for every minute of every day. So why not get a head start and do it before being asked?

Any company that is going to be successful in the long term is going to ask you to keep accurate records of your sales activity. I urge you to keep a chart for just two weeks that shows your activity. It will dramatically affect your life. You will discover (as I did) that little more than two hours per day are spent in actual revenue-producing activity. Most of the time is spent "getting ready" to participate in revenue-producing activity.

Top students sit down and *start* studying. Mediocre or poor students spend a lot of time *preparing* to study. Top salespeople do their planning and preparing during non-selling hours. When selling time comes, they pick up the phone, briefcase, or selling samples and start selling. In addition, the true "pros" in selling seize every opportunity—expected and unexpected—to sell, sell, sell!

A time log is not a limiting factor but a freeing factor. It will help you target the activities you need to add or delete. It also will indicate poor performance habits of which you are unaware.

THE DISCIPLINARIAN

Everyone needs a method, technique, or system for accountability. True professionals (in any and all activities) have the peace of mind that comes from knowing that they did the best they could with what they had at any given point in time. They feel confidence in knowing that they are being true to their personal values. This can be accomplished only with a system that allows the people seeking success to hold themselves accountable for tasks and objectives.

The Right System. You need some system for accountability. Ziglar Training Systems developed the Performance

Planner to help salespeople track tasks and results while planning objectives and providing specifics on setting short- and long-term goals to keep your life in balance. Other companies—such as Daytimers, Inc., and Franklin Covey—provide calendars, electronic devices, and concepts that allow you to make the best use of the time you have. A pencil and a piece of paper can be the beginnings of developing your personal performance tracking system. The most important thing is not which system you use—the most important thing is that you have a system. When sales professionals take the necessary steps to become even more organized and disciplined, they are taking steps toward maximum utilization of time and effort, which frees them in all areas of life!

SELLING 101—REAL MOTIVATION

Selling 101 was written to motivate you as a professional persuader. I hope that it showed you what you already know, gave you new information, and inspired you to combine the two so you will have new and even more creative ideas to enrich your career. If this book was helpful to you, then read *Ziglar On Selling* for a more in-depth exploration of these ideas and *Secrets of Closing the Sale* for those one hundred specific closes.

Now, if you begin using the ability you possess to apply these fundamental principles, I really will *See You Over the Top!*

Other Books by Zig Ziglar

Confessions of a Grieving Christian.
Nashville: Thomas Nelson, 1999.

Confessions of a Happy Christian. Gretna, La.: Pelican, 1978.

Courtship After Marriage: Romance Can Last a Lifetime.
Nashville: Thomas Nelson, 1990. Revised 2002.

Over the Top. Nashville: Thomas Nelson, 1997.

Raising Positive Kids in a Negative World.
Nashville: Thomas Nelson, 1985. Revised 2002.

See You at the Top. Gretna, La.: Pelican, 1974. Revised 2000.

Top Performance.
Old Tappan, N.J.: Fleming H. Revell Company, 1986.

Zig: The Autobiography of Zig Ziglar. New York: Doubleday, 2002.

Zig Ziglar's Secrets of Closing the Sale.
Old Tappan, N.J.: Fleming H. Revell Company, 1984.

Ziglar on Selling:
The Ultimate Handbook for the Complete Sales Professional.
Nashville: Thomas Nelson, 1991.

FOR YOUR CONTINUING EDUCATION

Guideposts.
Published monthly by Norman Vincent Peale and
Ruth Stafford Peale, Carmel, New York, 10512.

Harvard Business Review.
Published bimonthly by the Graduate School of Business
Administration, Boston, Massachusetts 02163.

Selling Power.
Published monthly by Gerhard Gschwandtner and Associates,
P.O. Box 5467, Fredericksburg, Virginia 22403.

Reader's Digest.
Published monthly by the Reader's Digest Association, Inc.,
Pleasantville, New York 10570.

ABOUT THE AUTHOR

A talented author and speaker, Zig Ziglar has an appeal that transcends barriers of age, culture, and occupation. Since 1970, he has traveled around the world delivering powerful life-improvement messages and cultivating the energy of change. A well-known authority on complete and balanced living, Mr. Ziglar has been recognized three times in the Congressional Record of the United States for his work with youth in the drug war and for his dedication to America.

Founder of Ziglar Training Systems, headquartered in Dallas, Texas, Mr. Ziglar has written twenty-two celebrated books on personal growth, leadership, sales, faith, family, and success, including *See You at the Top, Courtship after Marriage, Secrets of Closing the Sale, Success for Dummies,* and *Confessions of a Grieving Christian.* Nine titles have been on the bestseller lists, and his books and tapes have been translated into more than thirty-eight languages and dialects.